BEES IN AMBE[...] BOOK OF THO[...] VERSE BY JOHN OXENHAM PUBLISHED BY METHUEN & CO. 36 ESSEX STREET LONDON W.C. MDCCCCXIII

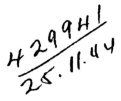

TO
THOSE
I HOLD DEAREST
THIS
OF MY BEST.

Published . . . . *September, 1913*
Reprinted . . . . *October, 1913*
Reprinted . . . . *October, 1913*
Reprinted . . . . *November, 1913*
Reprinted . . . . *November, 1913*
Reprinted . . . . *December, 1913*
Reprinted . . . . *December, 1913*
Reprinted . . . . *December, 1913*

Author's Apology

In these rushful days an apology is advisable, if not absolutely essential, from any man, save the one or two elect, who has the temerity to publish a volume of verse.

These stray lines, such as they are, have come to me from time to time, I hardly know how or whence; certainly not of deliberate intention or of malice aforethought. More often than not they have come to the interruption of other, as it seemed to me, more important—and undoubtedly more profitable—work.

They are, for the most part, simply attempts at concrete and rememberable expression of ideas—ages-old most of them—which ' asked for more.'

Most writers, I imagine, find themselves at times in that same predicament—worried by some thought which dances within them and stubbornly refuses to be satisfied with the sober dress of prose. For their own satisfaction and relief, in such a case, if they be not fools they endeavour to garb it more to its liking, and so find peace. Or, to vary the metaphor, they pluck the Bee out of their Bonnet and pop it into such amber as they happen to have about them or are able to evolve, and so put an end to its buzzing.

In their previous states these little Bonnet-Bees of mine have apparently given pleasure to quite a number of intelligent and thoughtful folk; and now—chiefly, I am bound to say, for my own satisfaction in seeing them all together—I have gathered them into one bunch.

If they please you—good! If not, there is no harm done, and one man is content.

JOHN OXENHAM.

CONTENTS

Credo

Not what, but **Whom**, I do believe,
   That, in my darkest hour of need,
   Hath comfort that no mortal creed
   To mortal man may give ;—
Not what, but **Whom** !
   For Christ is more than all the creeds,
   And His full life of gentle deeds
   Shall all the creeds outlive.
Not what I do believe, but **Whom** !
   Who walks beside me in the gloom?
   Who shares the burden wearisome ?
   Who all the dim way doth illume,
   And bids me look beyond the tomb
   The larger life to live ?—
Not what I do believe,
But **Whom** !
Not what,
But **Whom** !

Bees in Amber.

New Year's Day—and Every Day.

Each man is Captain of his Soul,
And each man his own Crew,
But the Pilot knows the Unknown Seas,
And He will bring us through.

We break new seas to-day,—
Our eager keels quest unaccustomed waters,
And, from the vast uncharted waste in front,
The mystic circles leap
To greet our prows with mightiest possi-
    bilities ;
Bringing us—what ?
    —Dread shoals and shifting banks ?
    —And calms and storms ?
    —And clouds and biting gales ?
    —And wreck and loss ?
    —And valiant fighting-times ?
And, maybe, Death !—and so, the Larger
    Life !

For should the Pilot deem it best
To cut the voyage short,
He sees beyond the sky-line, and
He'll bring us into Port.

And, maybe, Life,—Life on a bounding tide,
  And chance of glorious deeds ;—
  Of help swift-born to drowning mariners ;
  Of cheer to ships dismasted in the gale ;
  Of succours given unasked and joyfully ;
  Of mighty service to all needy souls.

So—Ho for the Pilot's orders,
Whatever course He makes !
For He sees beyond the sky-line,
And He never makes mistakes.

And, maybe, Golden Days,
    Full freighted with delight !
  —And wide free seas of unimagined bliss,
  —And Treasure Isles, and Kingdoms to
      be won,
  —And Undiscovered Countries, and New
    Kin.

For each man captains his own Soul,
And chooses his own Crew,
But the Pilot knows the Unknown Seas
And He will bring us through.

Philosopher's Garden.

" *See this my garden,*
    Large and fair ! "
—Thus, to his friend,
The Philosopher.

    " *'Tis not too long,*"
His friend replied,
With truth exact,—
    " *Nor yet too wide.*
    But well compact,
    If somewhat cramped
    On every side."

Quick the reply—
    " *But see how high !—*
    It reaches up
    To God's blue sky ! "

Not by their size
Measure we men
Or things.
Wisdom, with eyes
Washed in the fire,
Seeketh the things
That are higher—
Things that have wings,
Thoughts that aspire.

𝔉lowers of tbe 𝔇ust.

The Mills of God grind slowly, but they grind
    exceeding small——
So soft and slow the great wheels go they
    scarcely move at all ;
But the souls of men fall into them and are
    powdered into dust,
And in that dust grow the Passion-Flowers
    —Love, Hope, Trust.

Most wondrous their upspringing, in the dust
    of the Grinding-Mills,
And rare beyond the telling the fragrance
    each distils.
Some grow up tall and stately, and some grow
    sweet and small,
But Life out of Death is in each one—with
    purpose grow they all.

For that dust is God's own garden, and the
    Lord Christ tends it fair,
With oh, such loving tenderness ! and oh,
    such patient care !
In sorrow the seeds are planted, they are
    watered with bitter tears,
But their roots strike down to the Water-
    Springs and the Sources of the Years.

NOTE.—The first line only is adapted from the Sinnge-
dichte of Friedrich von Logau.

These flowers of Christ's own providence,
    they wither not nor die,
But flourish fair, and fairer still, through all
    eternity.
In the Dust of the Mills and in travail the
    amaranth seeds are sown,
But the Flowers in their full beauty climb
    the Pillars of the Throne.

The Pilgrim Way.

But once I pass this way,
And then—no more.
But once—and then, the Silent Door
Swings on its hinges,—
Opens . . . . closes,—
And no more
I pass this way.
So while I may,
With all my might,
I will essay
Sweet comfort and delight,
To all I meet upon the Pilgrim Way.
For no man travels twice
The Great Highway,
That climbs through Darkness up to Light,—
Through Night
To Day.

Everymaid.

King's Daughter !
Wouldst thou be all fair,
Without—within—
Peerless and beautiful,
A very Queen ?

Know then :—
Not as men build unto the Silent One,—
With clang and clamour,
Traffic of rude voices,
Clink of steel on stone,
And din of hammer ;—
Not so the temple of thy grace is reared.
But,—in the inmost shrine
Must thou begin,
And build with care
A Holy Place,
A place unseen,
Each stone a prayer.
Then, having built,
Thy shrine sweep bare
Of self and sin,
And all that might demean ;
And, with endeavour,
Watching ever, praying ever,
Keep it fragrant-sweet, and clean :
So, by God's grace, it be fit place,—
His Christ shall enter and shall dwell therein.

Not as in earthly fane—where chase
Of steel on stone may strive to win
Some outward grace,—
Thy temple face is chiselled from within.

Better and Best.

Better in bitterest agony to lie,
Before Thy throne,
Than through much increase to be lifted up
    on high,
And stand alone.

Better by one sweet soul, constant and true,
To be beloved,
Than all the kingdoms of delight to trample
    through,
Unloved, unloved.

Yet best—the need that broke me at Thy
    feet,
In voiceless prayer,
And cast my chastened heart, a sacrifice
    complete,
Upon Thy care.

For all the world is nought, and less than
    nought,
Compared with this,—
That my dear Lord, with His own life, my
    ransom bought,
And I am His.

D

⚓he ⚓haⱨow.

Shapeless and grim,
A Shadow dim
O'erhung the ways,
And darkened all my days.
And all who saw,
With bated breath,
Said, " It is Death ! "

And I, in weakness
Slipping towards the Night,
In sore affright
Looked up.   And lo ! —
No Spectre grim,
But just a dim
Sweet face,
A sweet high mother-face,
A face like Christ's Own Mother's face,
Alight with tenderness
And grace.

" Thou art not Death ! " I cried ;—
For Life's supremest fantasy
Had never thus envisaged Death to me ;—
"Thou art not Death, the End ! "

In accents winning,
Came the answer,—"*Friend,*
        There is no Death !
        I am the Beginning,
        — Not the End ! "

The Potter.

A Potter, playing with his lump of clay,
Fashioned an image of supremest worth.
    "Never was nobler image made on earth,
      Than this that I have fashioned of my
      clay.
    And I, of mine own skill, did fashion it,—
    I—from this lump of clay."

The Master, looking out on Pots and Men,
Heard his vain boasting, smiled at that he
said.
    " The clay is Mine, and I the Potter made,
      As I made all things,—stars, and clay,
      and men.
    In what doth this man overpass the rest ?
    —Be thou as other men ! "

He touched the Image,—and it fell to dust,
He touched the Potter,—he to dust did fall.
    Gently the Master,—" I did make them
      all,—
    All things and men, heaven's glories, and
      the dust.
    Who with Me works shall quicken death
      itself,
    Without Me—dust is dust."

Nightfall.

Fold up the tent !
The sun is in the West.
To-morrow my untented soul will range
Among the blest.
>   And I am well content,
>   For what is sent, is sent,
>   And God knows best.

Fold up the tent,
And speed the parting guest !
The night draws on, though night and day
   are one
On this long quest.
>   This house was only lent
>   For my apprenticement—
>   What is, is best.

Fold up the tent !
Its slack ropes all undone,
Its pole all broken, and its cover rent,—
Its work is done.
>   But mine—tho' spoiled and spent
>   Mine earthly tenement—
>   Is but begun.

Fold up the tent !
Its tenant would be gone,
To fairer skies than mortal eyes
May look upon.

All that I loved has passed,
And left me at the last
Alone !—alone !

Fold up the tent !
Above the mountain's crest,
I hear a clear voice calling, calling clear,—
" To rest ! To rest ! "
And I am glad to go,
For the sweet oil is low,
And rest is best !

The Pruner.

God is a zealous pruner,
For He knows——
Who, falsely tender, spares the knife
But spoils the rose.

The Ways.

To every man there openeth
A Way, and Ways, and a Way.
And the High Soul climbs the High way,
And the Low Soul gropes the Low,
And in between, on the misty flats,
The rest drift to and fro.
But to every man there openeth
A High Way, and a Low.
And every man decideth
The Way his soul shall go.

Seeds.

What shall we be like when
We cast this earthly body and attain
To immortality?}
What shall we be like then?

Ah, who shall say
What vast expansions shall be ours that day?
What transformations of this house of clay,
To fit the heavenly mansions and the light of
      day?
Ah, who shall say?

But this we know,—
We drop a seed into the ground,
A tiny, shapeless thing, shrivelled and dry,
And, in the fulness of its time, is seen
A form of peerless beauty, robed and crowned
Beyond the pride of any earthly queen,
Instinct with loveliness, and sweet and rare,
The perfect emblem of its Maker's care.

This from a shrivelled seed?—
—Then may man hope indeed!

For man is but the seed of what he shall be,
When, in the fulness of his perfecting,
He drops the husk and cleaves his upward
      way,
Through earth's retardings and the clinging
      clay,

Into the sunshine of God's perfect day.
No fetters then ! No bonds of time or space !
But powers as ample as the boundless grace
That suffered man, and death, and yet, in
    tenderness,
Set wide the door, and passed Himself
    before—
As He had promised—to prepare a place.

Yea, we may hope !
For we are seeds,
Dropped into earth for heavenly blossoming.
Perchance, when comes the time of harvest-
    ing,
His loving care
May find some use for even a humble tare.

We know not what we shall be—only this—
That we shall be made like Him—as He is.

Whirring Wheels.

Lord, when on my bed I lie,
Sleepless, unto Thee I'll cry ;
When my brain works overmuch,
Stay the wheels with Thy soft touch.

Just a quiet thought of Thee,
And of Thy sweet charity,—
Just a little prayer, and then
I will turn to sleep again.

The Bells of Ys.

When the Bells of Ys rang softly,—softly,
   Soft—and sweet—and low,
Not a sound was heard in the old gray town,
As the silvery tones came floating down,
 But life stood still with uncovered head,
And doers of ill did good instead,
And abroad the Peace of God was shed,
   When the bells aloft sang softly—softly,
    Soft—and sweet—and low,—
    The Silver Bells and the Golden Bells,—
    Aloft, and aloft, and alow.

And still those Bells ring softly—softly,
   Soft—and sweet—and low.
Though full twelve hundred years have gone,
Since the waves rolled over the old gray town,
Bold men of the sea, in the grip of the flow,
Still hear the Bells, as they pass and go,
Or win to life with their hearts aglow,
   When the Bells below sing softly—softly,
    Soft—and sweet—and low,—
    The Silver Bells and the Golden Bells,—
    Alow, and alow, and alow.

O the Mystical Bells, they still ring softly,
   Soft—and sweet—and low,—
For the sound of their singing shall never die
In the hearts that are tuned to their melody ;
And down in the world's wild rush and roar,
That sweeps us along to the Opening Door,

Hearts still beat high as they beat of yore,
When the Bells sing softly—softly—
softly,
Soft—and sweet—and low,
The Silver Bells and the Golden Bells,—
Alow, and aloft, and alow.

The Little Poem of Life.

I ;—
Thou ;—
We ;—
They ;—

Small words, but mighty.
In their span
Are bound the life and hopes of man.

For, first, his thoughts of his own self are full ;
Until another comes his heart to rule.
For them, life's best is centred round their
love ;
Till younger lives come all their love to prove.

Cup of Mixture.

For every Guest who comes with him to sup,
The Host compounds a strangely-mingled
cup ;—
Red Wine of Life and Dregs of Bitterness,
And, will-he nill-he, each must drink it up.

Weavers All.

Warp and Woof and Tangle,—
  Weavers of Webs are we.
Living and dying—and mightier dead,
For the shuttle, once sped, is sped—is sped ;—
  Weavers of Webs are we.

White, and Black, and Hodden-gray,—
  Weavers of Webs are we.
To every weaver one golden strand
Is given in trust by the Master-Hand ;—
  Weavers of Webs are we.

And that we weave, we know not,—
  Weavers of Webs are we.
The threads we see, but the pattern is known
To the Master-Weaver alone, alone ;—
  Weavers of Webs are we.

The Clearer Vision.

When, with bowed head,
And silent-streaming tears,
With mingled hopes and fears,
To earth we yield our dead ;
The Saints, with clearer sight,
Do cry in glad accord,—
" *A soul released from prison*
Is risen, is risen,—
Is risen to the glory of the Lord."

Shadows.

Shadows are but for the moment—
Quickly past ;
And then the sun the brighter shines
That it was overcast.

For Light is Life !
Gracious and sweet,
The fair life-giving sun doth scatter blessings
With his light and heat,—
And shadows.
But the shadows that come of the life-giving
     sun
Crouch at his feet.

No mortal life but has its shadowed times—
Not one !
Life without shadow could not taste the full
Sweet glory of the sun.

No shadow falls, but there, behind it, stands
The Light.
Behind the wrongs and sorrows of life's
     troublous ways
Stands RIGHT.

The Inn of Life.

As it was in the Beginning,—
Is Now,—
And . . . . ?

Anno Domini I.

————

" No room !
          No room !
The Inn is full,
Yea—overfull.
No room have we
For such as ye—
Poor folk of Galilee,
          Pass on ! Pass on ! "

" Nay then !—
Your charity
Will ne'er deny
Some corner mean,
Where she may lie unseen.
For see !—
Her time is nigh."

" Alack ! And she
So young and fair !
Place have we none ;
And yet—how bid ye gone ?
Stay then !—out there
Among the beasts
Ye may find room,

And eke a truss
To lie upon."

Anno Domini 1913, etc., etc.

———

  "No room!
    No room!
No room for Thee,
Thou Man of Galilee!
The house is full,
Yea, overfull.
There is no room for Thee,—
    Pass on! Pass on!

Nay—see!
The place is packed.
We scarce have room
For our own selves,
So how shall we
Find room for Thee,
Thou Man of Galilee,—
    Pass on! Pass on!

But—if Thou shouldst
This way again,
And we can find
So much as one small corner
Free from guest,
Not then in vain
Thy quest.
But now—
The house is full.
    Pass on!"

Save as Chiefest Guest.

Life's Chequer=Board.

"'Tis all a Chequer-Board of Nights and Days,
Where Destiny with men for pieces plays,
Hither and thither moves, and mates and slays,
And one by one back in the Closet lays."
Omar Khayyam.

A Chequer-Board of mingled Light and
 Shade ?
And We the Pieces on it deftly laid ?
Moved and removed, without a word to say,
By the Same Hand that Board and Pieces
 made ?

No Pieces we in any Fateful Game,
Nor free to shift on Destiny the blame ;
Each Soul doth tend its own immortal flame,
Fans it to Heaven, or smothers it in shame.

Cross=Roads.

Oft, as he jogs along the Winding-Way,
Occasion comes for Every Man to say,—
"This Road ?—— or That ? " and as he
 chooses then,
So shall his journey end in Night or Day.

Quo Vadis?

Peter, outworn,
And menaced by the sword,
Shook off the dust of Rome ;
And, as he fled,
Met one, with eager face,
Hastening cityward.
And, to his vast amaze,
It was The Lord.

"*Lord, whither goest Thou ?* "
He cried, importunate,
And Christ replied,—
"*Peter, I suffer loss.*
I go to take thy place,
To bear thy cross."

Then Peter bowed his head,
Discomforted ;
There, at the Master's feet,
Found grace complete,
And courage, and new faith,
And turned—with Him,
To Death.

So we,—
Whene'er we fail
Of our full duty,
Cast on Him our load,—
Who suffered sore for us,
Who frail flesh wore for us,
Who all things bore for us,—
On Christ, The Lord.

Tamate.

Great - Heart is dead, they say,—
Great-Heart the Teacher,
Great-Heart the Joyous,
Great-Heart the Fearless,
Great-Heart the Martyr,
Great-Heart of Sweet White Fire.

Great - Heart is dead, they say,—
Fighting the fight,
Holding the Light,
Into the night.
Great - Heart is dead, they say.—
But the Light shall burn the brighter,
And the night shall be the lighter,
For his going ;
And a rich, rich harvest for his sowing.

Great- Heart is dead, they say !—
What is death to such an one as Great-Heart ?
One sigh, perchance, for work unfinished
here ;—
Then a swift passing to a mightier sphere,
New joys, perfected powers, the vision
clear,
And all the amplitude of heaven to work
The work he held so dear.

Great - Heart is dead, say they ?
Nor dead nor sleeping ! He lives on ! His
name
Shall kindle many a heart to equal flame.

The fire he lighted shall burn on and on,
Till all the darkness of the lands be gone,
And all the kingdoms of the earth be won,
And one.

A soul so fiery sweet can never die,
But lives and loves and works through all
eternity.

Burden=Bearers.

Burden-bearers are we all,
Great and small.
Burden-sharers be ye all,
Great and small !
Where another shares the load,
Two draw nearer God.
Yet there are burdens we can share with none,
Save God ;
And paths remote where we must walk alone,
With God ;
For lonely burden and for path apart—
Thank God !
If these but serve to bring the burdened heart
To God.

The Iron Flail.

Time beats out all things with his iron flail,
Things great, things small.
With steady strokes that never fail,
With slow, sure strokes of his iron flail,
Time beats out all.

E

Sark.

Pearl Iridescent ! Pearl of the sea !
Shimmering, glimmering Pearl of the sea !
  White in the sun-flecked Silver Sea,
  White in the moon-decked Silver Sea,
  White in the wrath of the Silver Sea,—
Pearl of the Silver Sea !
  Lapped in the smile of the Silver Sea,
  Ringed in the foam of the Silver Sea,
  Glamoured in mists of the Silver Sea,—
Pearl of the Silver Sea !
  Glancing and glimmering under the sun,
  Jewel and casket all in one,
  Joy supreme of the sun's day dream,
  Soft in the gleam of the golden beam,—
Pearl of the Silver Sea !
  Splendour of Hope in the rising sun,
  Glory of Love in the noonday sun,
  Wonder of Faith in the setting sun,—
Pearl of the Silver Sea !

  Gaunt and grim to the outer world,
  Jewel and casket all impearled
  With the kiss of the Silver Sea !—
  With the flying kiss of the Silver Sea,
  With the long sweet kiss of the Silver Sea,
  With the rainbow kiss of the Silver Sea,—
Pearl of the Silver Sea !
  And oh the sight,—the wonderful sight,
  When calm and white, in the mystic light
  Of her quivering pathway, broad and
    bright,

The Queen of the Night, in silver dight,
Sails over the Silver Sea !

Wherever I go, and wherever I be,
The joy and the longing are there with me,—
The gleam and the glamour come back to me,—
In a mystical rapture there comes to me,
The call of the Silver Sea !
As needle to pole is my heart to thee,
Pearl of the Silver Sea !

E. A., Nov. 6, 1900.

Bright stars of Faith and Hope, her eyes
  Shall shine for us through all the years.
  For all her life was Love, and fears
Touch not the love that never dies.

And Death itself, to her, was but
  The wider opening of the door
  That had been opening, more and more,
Through all her life, and ne'er was shut.

—And never shall be shut. She left
  The door ajar for you and me,
  And, looking after her, we see
The glory shining through the cleft.

And when our own time comes,—again
  We'll meet her face to face ;—again
  We'll see the star-shine ; and again
She'll greet us with her soft, " Come ben ! "

The Passing of the Queen, January, 1901.

Hark ! The drums ! Muffled drums !
The long low ruffle of the drums !—
And every head is bowed,
In the vast expectant crowd,
As the Great Queen comes,—
    By the way she knew so well,
    Where our cheers were wont to swell,
    As we tried in vain to tell
    Of our love unspeakable.
Now she comes
To the rolling of the drums,
And the slow sad tolling of the bell.
Let every head be bowed,
In the silent waiting crowd,
As the Great Queen comes,
To the slow sad ruffle of the drums !

    Who is this that comes,
    To the rolling of the drums,
    In the sorrowful great silence of the peoples ?
Take heart of grace,
She is not here !
The Great Queen is not here !
    What most in her we did revere,—
    The lofty spirit, white and clear,
    The tender love that knew no fear,
    The soul sincere,—
These come not here,
To the rolling of the drums,
In the silence and the sorrow of the peoples.

Death has but little part
In her.   Love cannot die.
Who reigns in every heart
Hath immortality.
So, though our heads are bent
Our hearts are jubilant,
As she comes,—
As a conqueror she comes—
With the rolling of the drums,
To the stateliest of her homes,
In the hearts of her true and faithful peoples.
For the Great Queen lives for ever
In the hearts of those who love her.

The Golden Cord.

Through every minute of this day,
      Be with me, Lord !
Through every day of all this week,
      Be with me, Lord !
Through every week of all this year,
      Be with me, Lord !
Through all the years of all this life,
      Be with me, Lord !
So shall the days and weeks and years
Be threaded on a golden cord,
And all draw on with sweet accord
Unto Thy fulness, Lord,
That so, when time is past,
By Grace, I may at last,
      Be with Thee, Lord.

Thank God for Peace!
June, 1902.

Thank God for Peace !
Up to the sombre sky
Rolled one great thankful sigh,
Rolled one great gladsome cry—
The soul's deliverance of a mighty people.
Thank God for Peace !

The long-low-hanging war-cloud rolled away,
And night glowed brighter than the brightest
    day.
For Peace is Light,
And War is grimmer than the Night.

Thank God for Peace !
Great ocean was your mighty calm unstirred
As through your depths, unseen, unheard,
Sped on its way the glorious word
That called a weary nation to ungird,
And sheathed once more the keen, reluctant
    sword ?

Thank God for Peace !
The word came to us as we knelt in prayer
That wars might cease.
Peace found us on our knees, and prayer for
    Peace
Was changed to prayer of deepest thankful-
    ness.
We knelt in War, we rose in Peace to bless
Thy grace, Thy care, Thy tenderness.

Thank God for Peace !

No matter now the rights and wrongs of it ;
You fought us bravely, and we fought you
  fair.
The fight is done. Grip hands ! No malice
  bear !
We greet you, brothers, to the nobler strife
Of building up the newer, larger life !

Join hands ! Join hands ! Ye nations of the
  stock !
And make henceforth a mighty Trust for
  Peace ;—
A great enduring peace that shall withstand
The shocks of time and circumstance ; and
  every land
Shall rise and bless you—and shall never
  cease
To bless you—for that glorious gift of Peace.

God's Handwriting.

He writes in characters too grand
For our short sight to understand ;
We catch but broken strokes, and try
To fathom all the mystery
Of withered hopes, of death, of life,
The endless war, the useless strife,—
But there, with larger, clearer sight,
We shall see this—His way was right.

Stephen—Saul.

Stephen, who died while I stood by con-
    senting,
  Wrought in his death the making of a life,
Bruised one hard heart to thought of swift
    repenting,
  Fitted one fighter for a nobler strife.

Stephen, the Saint, triumphant and forgiving,
  Prayed while the hot blows beat him to the
    earth.
Was that a dying ? Rather was it living !—
  Through his soul's travail my soul came to
    birth.

Stephen, the Martyr, full of faith and fearless,
  Smiled when his bruised lips could no
    longer pray,—
Smiled with a courage undismayed and peer-
    less,—
  Smiled !—and that smile is with me, night
    and day.

O, was it *I* that stood there, all consenting ?
  I—at whose feet the young men's clothes
    were laid ?
Was it *my* will that wrought that hot tor-
    menting ?
  My heart that boasted over Stephen, dead ?

Yes, it was I. And sore to me the telling.
Yes, it was I. And thought of it has been
God's potent spur my whole soul's might
 compelling
These outer darknesses for Him to win.

Paul.

Bond-slave to Christ, and in my bonds rejoic-
 ing,
 Earmarked to Him I counted less than
 nought ;
His man henceforward, eager to be voicing
 That wondrous Love which Saul the
 Roman sought.

Sought him and found him, working bitter
 sorrow ;
 Found him and claimed him, chose him for
 his own ;
Bound him in darkness, till the glorious
 morrow
Unsealed his eyes to that he had not known.

Wakening.

This mortal dies,—
But, in the moment when the light fails here,
The darkness opens, and the vision clear
Breaks on his eyes.
The vail is rent,—
On his enraptured gaze heaven's glory breaks,
He was asleep, and in that moment wakes.

Macedonia, 1903.

Devils' work !
Devils' work, my masters !
   Britain, your hands are red !
You may close your heart but you cannot
  shirk
This terrible fact,—*We—kept—the—Turk.*
His day was past and we knew his work,
But he played our game so we kept the Turk,
For our own sake's sake we kept the Turk.
   Britain, your hands are red !

Red are the walls and the ways,
   And—Britain, your hands are red !
There is blood on the hearth, and blood in the
  well,
And the whole fair land is a red, red hell,—
   Britain, your hands are red !

"*Come over ! Come over and help us !*"
We are deaf to the ancient cry.
—"*For the sake of our women and children !*"
And Britain stands quietly by.
   O Britain, your hands are red !

Cleanse your hands, Britain !
Yea, cleanse them in blood if it *must* be !
For blood that is shed in the cause of right
Has power, as of old, to wash souls white.
   Cleanse your hands, Britain !

O for the fiery grace of old,—
The heart and the masterful hand !
But grace grows dim and the fire grows cold,
We are heavy with greed and lust and gold,
And life creeps low in the land.

Break your bonds, Britain !
Stand up once again for the right !
We have stained our hands in the times that
   are past,
Before God, we would wash them white.

For the Nations are in the proving ;
Each day is Judgment Day ;
And the peoples He finds wanting
Shall pass—by the winding way.

Ibearts in Exile.

O Exiled Hearts—for you, for you—
Love still can find the way !
   Hear the voices of the women on the road !
O Shadowed Lives—for you, for you—
Hope hath not lost her ray !
   Hear the laughter of the children on the
   road !
O Gloomy Night—for you, for you—
Dawn tells of coming day !
   Hear the clink of breaking fetters on the
   road !
O Might sans Right—for you, for you—
The feet of crumbling clay !
   Hear the slow, sure tread of Freedom on
   the road !

Wandered.

The wind blows shrill along the hill,
—*Black is the night and cold*—
The sky hangs low with its weight of snow,
And the drifts are deep on the wold.
But what care I for wind or snow ?
And what care I for the cold ?
　　　　Oh . . . where is my lamb—
　　　　My one ewe lamb—
　　　　That strayed from the fold ?

The beasts are safely gathered in,
—*Black is the night and cold*—
They are snug and warm, and safe from harm,
In stall and byre and fold.
And the dogs and I, by the blazing fire,
Care nought for the snow and the cold.
　　　　Oh . . . where is my lamb—
　　　　My one ewe lamb—
　　　　That strayed from the fold ?

The barns are bursting with their store
Of grain like yellow gold ;
A full, fat year has brought good cheer,
—*Black is the night and cold.*—
But . . . What care I for teeming barns ?
And what care I for gold ?
　　　　Oh . . . where is my lamb—
　　　　My one ewe lamb—
　　　　That strayed from the fold ?

In the great kitchen, maids and men,
—*Black is the night and cold*—
Laugh loud and long, with jest and song,
And merry revel hold.
Let them laugh and sing, let them have their
    fling,
But for me—I am growing old.
       Oh . . . where is my lamb—
      My one ewe lamb—
      That strayed from the fold?

The old house moans, and sighs and groans,
—*Black is the night and cold*—
We have seen brave times, you and I, old
    friend,
But now—we are growing old.
We have stood foursquare to many a storm,
But now—we are growing old.
       Oh . . . where is my lamb—
      My one ewe lamb—
      That strayed from the fold?

Her mother sleeps on the hill out there,
—*Black is the night and cold,*—
She is free from care, she is happier there,
Beneath the warm brown mould.
And I've sometimes hoped they may have
    met,
And the end of the tale be told.
       Ah . . . where is our lamb—
      Our one ewe lamb—
      That strayed from the fold?

Was that a branch that shed its load ?
—*Black is the night and cold,*—
Or—was it a footstep in the snow—
A timid footstep—halting, slow ?
Ah me ! I am getting old !
Is that a tapping—soft and low ?
Can it be . . . I thought I heard . . . but
   no,
'Twas only a branch that shed its snow,—
God's truth ! I am getting old !
     For I thought . . . maybe
     It was my lamb
     Come home again to the fold.

Dear Lord !—a hand at the frozen pane !
—*White on the night's black cold*—
O my lamb ! my lamb ! are you come again ?
My dear lost lamb, are you come again ?
Are you come again to the fold ?
It is ! . . . It is ! . . . Now I thank Thee,
   Lord,
For Thy Mercies manifold !
     She is come again !
     She is home again !
     My lamb that strayed from the fold !

Bide a Wee !

Though the times be dark and dreary,
Though the way be long,
Keep your spirits bright and cheery,—
—" Bide a wee, and dinna weary ! "
   Is a heartsome song.

The Word that was left Unsaid.

" A red rose for my helmet,
And a word before we part !
The rose shall be my oriflamme
The word shall fill my heart."
Heart, Heart, Heart of my heart—
Just a look, just a word and a look !
A look or a sign that my love shall divine
And a word for my hungering heart !

She toyed with his love and her roses ;
Was it mischief or mischance ?—
She dropped him a rose—'twas a white one,
And he lifted it on his lance.
Heart, Heart, Heart of my heart !
Is it thus—is it thus we part ?
With never a look, and never a sign,
Nor a word for my hungering heart !

She sought him among the dying,
She found him among the dead ;
And the rose was still in his helmet,
But his life had stained it red.
Heart, Heart, Heart of my heart !
Now my heart within me is dead.
And alack for the look !
And alas for the sign !
And the word that was left unsaid !

Don't Worry.

Just do your best,
And leave the rest
To Him who gave you
Life,—
And Zeal for Labour,—
And the Joy of Strife,—
And Zest of Love,—
And all that lifts your soul above
The lower things.

Life's truest harvest is in what we *would*,
And strive our best for,
Not most in what we *could*.
The things we count supreme
Stand, haply, not so high
In God's esteem
As *How* and *Why*.

All-Seeing Sight
Cleaves through the husk of things,
Right to the Roots and Springs,—
Sees all things whole,
And measures less the body than the soul.
All-Righteous Right
Will weigh men's motives,
Not their deeds alone.
End and Beginning unto Him are one;
And *would* for *could* shall oft, perchance,
    atone.

Motives are seeds,
From which at times spring deeds
Not equal to the soul's outreaching hope.
Strive for the stars !
Count nought well done but best !
Then, with brave patience, leave the rest
To Him who knows.
He'll judge you justly ere the record close.

The Golden Rose.

The Golden Rose is blowing still,
  Is growing still, is glowing still,
In lowly vale, on lordly hill,
The Golden Rose is blowing still ;—
  If only you can find it !

The Golden Rose still breaks and blows,
  Still breaks and blows, still gleams and
    glows,
'Mid icy blasts, and wintry snows,
The Golden Rose still breaks and blows ;—
  Search well and you may find it !

The Golden Rose can never die,
  'Tis grafted on Eternity ;
In hearts that Love doth glorify,
The Golden Rose can never die,—
  May it be yours to find it !

F

Gadara, A.D. 31.

Rabbi, begone ! Thy powers
Bring loss to us and ours.
Our ways are not as Thine.
Thou lovest men, we—swine.
Oh, get you hence, Omnipotence,
And take this fool of Thine !
His soul ? What care we for his soul ?
What good to us that Thou has made him
    whole,
Since we have lost our swine ?

And Christ went sadly.
He had wrought for them a sign
Of Love, and Hope, and Tenderness divine ;
They wanted—swine.
Christ stands without *your* door and gently
    knocks ;
But if your gold, or swine, the entrance
    blocks,
He forces no man's hold—he will depart,
And leave you to the treasures of your heart.

No cumbered chamber will the Master share,
But one swept bare
By cleansing fires, then plenished fresh and
    fair
With meekness, and humility, and prayer.
There will He come, yet, coming, even there
He stands and waits, and will no entrance win
Until the latch be lifted from within.

The Bells of Stepan Iline.

(Cradle Song from "The Long Road.")

Whisht, Baby! Whisht!
Quick below the cover!
Down into your nest, my bird!
And—don't—you—dare—peep—over!
For the grey wolves they are prowling,
They are prowling, they are prowling.
And the snow-wind it is howling,
It is howling, it is howling.
Hark!---- Hark!----
Out there in the dark—
Ow---ooh! Ow---ooh!
S-s-s-s-s-seee--oo--ooh!
The wolves they are lean,
So-o-o lean, so-o-o lean!
And the wind it is keen,
So-o-o keen, so-o-o keen!
And they seek little babies who aren't sleeping!
But lie you still, my Baby dear!
Lie still, lie still, and maybe you'll hear—
Hark!---- Hark!----
Out there in the dark,—
The silver bells and the golden bells,
The swinging bells and the singing bells,—
The bells that are heard but never are seen.
The wind and the wolves, and the bells in
      between,—
The bells of Iline,
Good Stepan Iline,—
The bells of good Stepan
Iline!

Bolt that Door!

Each sin has its door of entrance.
Keep—that—door—closed !
Bolt it tight !
Just outside, the wild beast crouches
In the night.
Pin the bolt with a prayer,
God will fix it there.

Giant Circumstance.

Though every nerve be strained
To fine accomplishment,
Full oft the life falls spent
Before the prize is gained.
And, in our discontent
At waste so evident,
In doubt and vast discouragement
We wonder what is meant.
But, tracing back, we find
A Power that held the ways—
A Mighty Hand, a Master Mind,
That all the troubled course defined,
And overruled the days.
Some call it Fate ; some—Chance ;
Some—Giant Circumstance ;
And some, upreaching to the sense
Of God within the circumstance,
Do call it—Providence !

The Hungry Sea.

Down to the sea, the hungry sea,
    O the sea is hungry ever !
Seeking food for the bairns and me,
Seeking food in the hungry sea ;
    O the sea is hungry ever !

My man and my lad—their bones are white,
    O the sea is hungry ever !
Into the maw of the grim black night,
Their hearts were bold and their faces bright ;
    O the sea is hungry ever !

The sun was red and the clouds were black,
    O the sea is hungry ever !
And the sky was heavy with flying wrack,
When forth they fared,—and they came not
    back ;
    O the sea is hungry ever !

Forth they fared and they came not back,
    O the sea is hungry ever !
O, I fear the sea, and I hate the sea,
That took my man and my lad from me ;
    O the sea is hungry ever !

We Thank Thee, Lord.

We thank Thee, Lord,
That of Thy tender grace,
In our distress
Thou hast not left us wholly comfortless.

We thank Thee, Lord,
That of Thy wondrous might,
Into our night
Thou hast sent down the glory of the Light.

We thank Thee, Lord,
That all Thy wondrous ways,
Through all our days,
Are Wisdom, Right, and Ceaseless Tender-
  ness.

The Vail.

He only sees both sides of that dark vail
That hangs before men's eyes—
He only. It is well !
Hope ever stands unseen
Behind the screen,
For knowledge would bring Hope to sudden
  death,
And cloud the present with the coming ill.
I would lie still, Dear Lord,
I would lie still,
And stay my troubled heart on Thee,
Obedient to Thy will.

No East or West.

In Christ there is no East or West,
  In Him no South or North,
But one great Fellowship of Love
  Throughout the whole wide earth.

In Him shall true hearts everywhere
  Their high communion find.
His service is the golden cord
  Close-binding all mankind.

Join hands then, Brothers of the Faith,
  Whate'er your race may be !—
Who serves my Father as a son
  Is surely kin to me.

In Christ now meet both East and West,
  In Him meet South and North,
All Christly souls are one in Him,
  Throughout the whole wide earth.

The Day—The Way.

Not for one single day
Can I discern my way,
    But this I surely know,—
Who gives the day,
Will show the way.
    So I securely go.

Liberty, Equality, Fraternity.

O God, within whose sight
All men have equal right
    To worship Thee.
Break every bar that holds
Thy flock in diverse folds !
Thy Will from none withholds
    Full liberty.

Lord, set Thy Churches free
From foolish rivalry !
    Lord, set us free !
Let all past bitterness
Now and for ever cease
And all our souls possess
    Thy charity !

Lord, set the people free !
Let all men draw to Thee
    In unity !
Thy temple courts are wide,
Therein let all abide
In peace, and side by side,
    Serve only Thee !

God, grant us now Thy peace !
Bid all dissensions cease !
    God, send us peace !
Peace in True Liberty,
Peace in Equality,
Peace and Fraternity,
    God, send us peace !

Freemen.

Let no man stand between my God and me !
I claim a Free man's right
Of intercourse direct with Him,
Who gave me Freedom with the air and light.
God made me free.—
Let no man stand between
Me and my liberty !

We need no priest to tell us God is Love.—
Have we not eyes to see,
And minds to apprehend, and hearts
That leap responsive to His Charity ?
God's gifts are free.—
Let no man stand between
Us and His liberty !

We need no priest to point a way to heaven.—
God's heaven is here,—is there,—
Man's birthright, with the light and air,—
" God is His own and best interpreter."
His ways are free.—
Let no man stand between
Us and His liberty !

Let no man strive to rob us of this right !
For this, from age to age,
Our fathers did a mighty warfare wage,
And, by God's help, we'll keep our heritage
God says—" Be Free ! "
And we,—
" No Man shall stand between
Our Sons and Liberty ! "

The Long Road.

Long the road,
　　Till Love came down it !
Dark the life,
　　Till Love did crown it !
Dark the life,
　　And long the road,
Till Love came
　　To share the load !
For the touch
　　Of Love transfigures
All the road
　　And all its rigours.
Life and Death
　　Love's touch transfigures.
Life and Death,
　　And all that lies
In between,
　　Love sanctifies.
Once the heavenly spark is lighted,
Once in love two hearts united.
Nevermore
　　Shall aught that was be
As before.

The Christ.

The good intent of God became the Christ,
And lived on earth—the Living Love of God,
That men might draw to closer touch with
　　heaven,
Since Christ in all the ways of man hath trod.

The Ballad of Lost Souls.

With the thirty pieces of silver,
They bought the Potter's Field ;
For none would have the blood-money
And the interest it might yield.

The Place of Blood for the Price of Blood,
And that was meet, I ween,
For there they would bury the dead who died
In frowardness and sin.

And the first man they would bury there
Was Judas Iscariot ;
And that was as dreadful a burying
As ever was, I wot.

For the sick earth would not keep him ;
Each time it thrust him out,
And they that would have buried him
Stood shuddering round about.

And others they would bury
In that unhallowed spot,
But honest earth would none of them,
Because of Iscariot.

And oh, it was a fell, fell place,
With dead black trees all round,
And a quag that boiled and writhed and coiled
Where had been solid ground.

For every tree that stood there,
And the green grass every blade,
Shrivelled and died on every side,
Whenever the price was paid.

And in despair they left him there,
And there his body lay,
Till his sad soul came, all black with shame,
And carried it away.

And those denied a sepulture
In that most dismal spot,
Gibbered and flew, a ghastly crew,
Incensed with rage, that grew and grew,
Against Iscariot.

For their souls were all in torment,
While their bodies uncovered lay,
And never a moment's rest was theirs,
Either by night or day.

That was a place of wailings,
And the grisly things of Death,—
The bare black arms of the trees above,
And the black quag underneath.

No light of the moon fell on it,
Nor ever a star did shine
On the quivering face of that dread place,
Because of Iscariot's sin.

Then there came by the soul of Iscariot,
The same who sold his Lord,
And he dragged his body after him,
But never spake a word.

Since earth his body would not,
He must drag it to and fro,
He had tried in vain to be quit of it,
But it would not let him go.

So the soul of Judas Iscariot
Came by the Potter's Field,
And there the ill his deed had wrought
Was unto him revealed.

And when the others saw him,
They leaped at him eagerly ;—
"This is he for whom we suffer !
—'Tis he ! 'Tis he ! 'Tis he !"

Then all afire with mad desire,
They chased him through the dark,
And each soul carried his dead bodie,
Grim, and stiff, and stark.

They struck at him with their bodies,
They cursed him for his sin,
They made to tear his dumb soul there,
With their fingers long and lean.

And Judas fled in his horror,
With that fell crew behind,

And as they sped the people said
Death rode upon the wind.

They chased him near, they chased him far,
Because of his treachery,
And ever he just escaped their lust,
And ever they were nigh.

They chased him near, they chased him far,
And ever they were nigh,
And never a star shone out on them
Out of the cold black sky.

And as they sped by Calvary,
There were empty crosses three,—
And on the ground, below the mound,
Lay one in agony.

"Three times I swore I knew him not,
And then—he looked on me.
Ah, such a look !—no harshest word
Had ever proved so sharp a sword
To my inconstancy.

"Three times I did deny Thee, Lord !
And yet, thou couldst forgive,
Now am I thine—in life, in death ;
Thee will I serve with every breath,
While I have breath to give."

They sped by an open window,
Where one knelt all alone

In great amaze, in greater grief,
In woe that wrestled with belief,
The Mother mourned her Son.

"*My son, I knew thee more than man,*—
Ah me !—and the heart of me !
Yet, man in God, and God in man,
Still wast thou part of me.

"*The nails through thy dear hands and feet,*—
Ah me ! they pierced my own.
The thorns that on thy brow they plied,—
The spear they drove into thy side,—
The pangs thy Godhead could not hide,—
They pierced me too, my son.

"*My son ! My son ! My more than son,*
My heart is full for thee !
Yet, tho' I know thee so much more
Than ever mortal man before,—
Yea, tho' I worship and adore,—
Woe's me !—and the heart of me !"

And ever they came by the Potter's Field,
And thrust their bodies in,
And ever the sick earth spat them out,
Because of Iscariot's sin.

They sped along a palace-wall,
The feast waxed high inside,—
On Golgotha the Cross still stood,
The Cross where man had nailed his God,

Red was the Rood still with his blood,—
They drank—"*The Crucified !*"

The revel gashed the sombre night,
And fast the wine-cups plied,—
Time touched Eternity that day ;—
God had come down to man that day ;—
The world began anew that day ;—
They drank—"*The Crucified !*"

And ever again to the Potter's Field,
The Souls in torment came,
But the black quag boiled and writhed and
        coiled,
And would have none of them.

And everywhere strange shapes of death
Walked in the fearsome gloom,
For that last cry from Calvary
Had rent in twain the Temple vail,
And burst the gates of Doom.

Through all the startled city, walked
The saints that had been dead,
And to the sorrowful in heart
Holy comfort ministrèd.

And when they met Iscariot,
Sore hounded in the chase,
They cried to him, for the Love of God,
To seek God's grace.

And ever to the Field of Death,
The souls in torment came,
Seeking the rest of the Blessèd Dead,—
But Earth would none of them.

And as they whirled through a garden,
They came on an empty tomb,
The stone was gone, a soft light shone
Full softly on the gloom.

Bright was that Light, and wondrous bright,
'Twas brighter than the sun ;
As then it shone, so shines it now,
And shall when Time is done.

And all along the pathway
Was a track of throbbing light ;
Where the Christ had gone his footsteps shone,
Like stars in a velvet night.

'Twas the spent soul of Iscariot
Was like the wind-blown dust,
As nearer still, and near, and near,
He bent and crept, in doubt, and fear,
He came because he must.

'Twas the sick soul of Iscariot
That drew from out the night,
And the full of his sin was known to him
In the Shining of the Light.

G

In the rim of the Light he laid him,
Repented of his sin.
" *I wotted not !   I wotted not !*
Dear Master, take me in ! "

And as he lay there sorrowing,
Up came the felon crew.
They flailed him with their dead bodỳs,
They heeded not his rue.

They flailed him with their dead bodỳs,
He heeded not their spleen.
" *I wotted not !   I wotted not !*
Dear Master, take me in ! "

And then . . . a Vision and a Voice,—
And the Word made manifest,—
"*Lay down thy load where I abode,*
And I will give thee rest !

" *And ye,—no more hunt Iscariot !*
He repents him of his sin.
And never a soul that repenteth
But he may enter in.

"*This Day the Door is opened*
That shall never close again,
And never a soul that would come in
Shall seek to come in vain."

So the dead soul of Iscariot
Was born again that night ;
For the Lord Christ came dead souls to claim
And lead them into Light.

And the souls of the unburied,
When they looked upon His face,
Were cleansed of sin and entered in
To His redeeming grace.

So, by that wonderful great Love
Which highest heaven extols,—
To Mother Earth their dead bodies,
And unto Christ their souls.

Profit and Loss.

Profit ?—Loss ?
Who shall declare this good—that ill ?—
When good and ill so intertwine
But to fulfil the vast design
Of an Omniscient Will ?—
When seeming gain but turns to loss,—
When earthly treasure proves but dross,—
And what seemed loss but turns again
To high, eternal gain ?

Wisest the man who does his best,
And leaves the rest
To Him who counts not deeds alone,
But sees the root, the flower, the fruit
And calls them one.

Free Men of God.

Free men of God, the New Day breaks
In golden gleams across the sky ;
The darkness of the night is past,
This is the Day of Victory.
 For this our fathers strove
 In stern and fiery love—
 That men to come should be
 Born into liberty—
That all should be—as we are—Free !

Free men of God, gird up your loins,
And brace you for the final fight !
Strike home, strike home for Truth and Right :
—Yet bear yourselves as in His sight !
 For this our fathers fought,
 This with their lives they bought—
 That you and I should be
 Heirs of their liberty—
That all should be—as we are—Free !

Free men we are and so will be ;
We claim free access unto Him,
Who widened all the bounds of life,
And us from bondage did redeem.
 Let no man intervene,
 Or draw a veil between
 Us and our God, for He
 Would have His people free,—
And we would be—as Thou art—Free.

Free men of God, your Birthright claim !
Our fathers won it with a price.
They paid in full to axe and flame,
Nor counted up the sacrifice.
    This is our heritage,
    And here we do engage,
    Each man unto his son
    Intact to pass it on.
So shall they be—as we are—Free !

Our Sure Defence, in times of stress,
Thy gates stand open, wide and free,
When men provoke and wrongs oppress,
We seek Thy wider liberty.
    With loftier mind and heart,
    Let each man bear his part !
    So—to the final fight,
    And God defend the right !
We shall, we must, we will be—Free !

Treasure Trove.

Lord Christ, let me but hold Thy hand
And all the rest may go.
For nothing is, but only seems,
And life is full of idle dreams,
    Until Thyself we know.

The whole wide world is nought beside
The wonder of Thy love.
And though my state be mean and strait,
Give me but heart to work and wait,
    And I have Treasure-Trove.

The Gate.

"A little child shall lead them."

I trod an arduous way, but came at last
To where the city walls rose fair and white
Above the darkening plain,—a goodly sight.
And eagerly, while yet a great way off,
My eyes did seek the Gates—the Great White
    Gates
That close not ever, day or night, but stand
Wide as the love of Christ that opened them.
But nought could I discern of gate or breach,
The wall stood flawless far as eye could reach.

But when I drew in closer to the wall,
I saw a lowly portal, strait and small;
So small, a man might hardly enter there,
Low-browed and shadowed, and close-pressed
    to earth—
A very needle's eye—scarce visible.
I looked and wondered.   Could this trivial
    way
Be the sole entrance to the light of day?
And as I stood perplext, a clear voice cried,—
"*Come!   Enter in!   The Gate is open wide.*"

And while I stood in doubt, there came along
One of earth's mighty ones—a conqueror
Of Kings.   He looked for gates that should
    swing wide
To meet his high estate and welcome him.

He stood and gazed, then raised his voice and
    cried,
" My work on earth is done. I would within."
And from the City wall the voice replied,—
"*Come ! Enter in ! The Gate is open wide.*"
He stood perplext, then set himself to wait,
Till Might should help him to discern the Gate.

Another came,—a man of mind so rare,
He scarce had breathed the common earthly
    air.
Knowledge was his, and wisdom so profound,
All things he knew in heaven and earth. No
    bound
To his accomplishment, until he sought
The great wide-opened Gate,—and found it
    not.
He stood perplext, and then cried wearily,
" Pray give me entrance. I am done with
    earth."
And from the City wall the clear voice cried,—
"*Come ! Enter in ! The Gate is open wide.*"
He looked in vain, then set himself to wait,
Till Wisdom should direct him to the gate.

I saw a woman come, noble and fair,
And pure of heart, and in her goodly deeds
More richly robed than Fashion's fairest
    queen.
And to myself I said,—" Surely for her
A way will open that she may go in ! "

She said no word, but stood and looked upon
The shining walls, with eyes that answering
        shone.
And from the City wall the clear voice cried,—
"*Come ! Enter in ! The Gate is open wide.*"
She looked in vain, then set herself to wait,
Till Love should help her to discern the Gate.

And one there came, with clear keen face—a
        Judge
Of men on earth, and famed for fearless truth.
His robes were stainless and his heart was
        clean.
" Entrance I crave," he cried, " to well-
        earned rest,—
And mercy-tempered justice and no more."
And from the City wall the clear voice cried,—
"*Come ! Enter in ! The Gate is open wide.*"
He looked in vain, then set himself to wait
Till Judgment should direct him to the Gate.

And one there came, sad-eyed, his brow still
        raw
From pressure of an earthly crown. He too
Sought glorious entrance through wide-
        opened gates,
And stood perplext. He had borne well his
        part,
And served his people and his God, and died
The Martyr's death, and yet he found no gate.
" I fain would rest," he cried. " My life has
        been

One ceaseless striving. I would enter in."
And from the City wall the clear voice cried—
"*Come ! Enter in ! The Gate is open wide.*"
Perplext he stood, then set himself to wait,
Till Patient Waiting should discern the Gate.

And one who had had riches beyond most,
And yet subserved them to his Master's good,
Came searching for the heavenly gates, and
   stood
Amazed to find no opening in the walls.
" I gave of all I had," he cried, " and held
Nought as my own,—yet entrance is denied."
And from the City wall the clear voice cried,—
"*Come ! Enter in ! The Gate is open wide.*"
He stood perplext, then set himself to wait
Till Charity should point him to the Gate.

And many more there were who entrance
   craved,
And sought the Great White Gates, and stood
   perplext.
And ever, from within, the clear voice cried,—
"*Come ! Enter in ! The Gate is open wide.*"
They sought in vain, and set themselves to
   wait
Till Light was given them to discern the Gate.

And then—a child in white came carolling
Along the arduous road we all had trod.
He stopped and looked, then laughed with
   childish glee,—

*" Why wait ye here without ? Come, follow
    me ! "*—
And passed, scarce bending, through the
    lowly door,—
We heard his singing,—him we saw no more.

The woman stooped and looked, with eyes
    that shone,
Into the doorway where the child had gone ;
Then loosed her robes and dropped, and in a
    shift
Of pure white samite, on her hands and knees
She crept into the doorway and was gone,
And we stood gazing at the way she went.

And, one by one, they followed. First the
    Judge
Laid by his robes, and bowed him to the
    ground,
And followed—where the little child had led.
And he whose brow had borne that weighty
    crown
Bent low and followed,—where the little child
    had led.
And he who knew so much of earthly things
Discarded them, and, on his hands and knees,
Crept through the doorway,—where the little
    child had led.
And he of riches laid him in the dust
And followed,—where the little child had led.
And, last of all, the War Lord cast aside
His victor's wreaths, and all his pomp and
    pride,

And followed,—where the little child had led.
And, groping through my fears, I bowed my
    head
And followed,—where the little child had led.

Bring Us the Light.

I hear a clear voice calling, calling,
Calling out of the night,
O, you who live in the Light of Life,
    Bring us the Light !

We are bound in the chains of darkness,
Our eyes received no sight,
O, you who have never been bond or blind,
    Bring us the Light !

We live amid turmoil and horror,
Where might is the only right,
O, you to whom life is liberty,
    Bring us the Light !

We stand in the ashes of ruins,
We are ready to fight the fight,
O, you whose feet are firm on the Rock,
    Bring us the Light !

You cannot—you shall not forget us,
Out here in the darkest night,
We are drowning men, we are dying men,
    Bring, O, bring us the Light !

All's Well !

Is the pathway dark and dreary ?
  God's in His heaven !
Are you broken, heart-sick, weary ?
  God's in His heaven !
Dreariest roads shall have an ending,
Broken hearts are for God's mending.
      All's well ! All's well !
        All's . . . well !

Are life's threads all sorely tangled ?
  God's in His heaven !
Are the sweet chords strained and jangled ?
  God's in His heaven !
Tangled threads are for Love's fingers,
Trembling chords make heaven's sweet
    singers.
      All's well ! All's well !
        All's . . . well !

Is the burden past your bearing ?
  God's in His heaven !
Hopeless ?—Friendless ?—No one caring ?
  God's in His heaven !
Burdens shared are light to carry,
Love shall come though long He tarry.
      All's well ! All's well !
        All's . . . well !

Is the light for ever failing ?
    God's in His heaven !
Is the faint heart ever quailing ?
    God's in His heaven !
God's strong arms are all around you,
In the dark He sought and found you.
      All's well ! All's well !
        All's . . . well !

Is the future black with sorrow ?
    God's in His heaven !
Do you dread each dark to-morrow ?
    God's in His heaven !
Nought can come without His knowing.
Come what may 'tis His bestowing.
      All's well ! All's well !
        All's . . . well !

Peace and heaven lie all about us.
    God's in His heaven !
Peace within makes heaven without us.
    God's in His heaven !
God's great love shall fail us never,
We are His, and His for ever.
      All's well ! All's well !
        All's . . . well !

ꜩis Mercy Endureth for Ever.

Our feet have wandered, wandered far and
      wide,—
    His Mercy endureth for ever !
From that strait path in which the Master
      died,—
    His Mercy endureth for ever !
Low have we fallen from our high estate,
Long have we lingered, lingered long and late;
      But the tenderness of God
      Is from age to age the same,
      And His Mercy endureth for ever !

There is no sin His Love can not forgive ;—
    His Mercy endureth for ever !
No soul so stained His Love will not receive ;
    His Mercy endureth for ever !
No load of sorrow but His touch can move,
No hedge of thorns that can withstand His
      Love ;
      For the tenderness of God
      Is from age to age the same,
      And His Mercy endureth for ever !

So we will sing, whatever may betide ;—
    His Mercy endureth for ever !
Nought but ourselves can keep us from His
      side ;—
    His Mercy endureth for ever !
What though no place we win in life's rough
      race,

Our loss may prove the measure of His grace.
For the tenderness of God
Is from age to age the same,
And His Mercy endureth for ever !

God is Good.

I faced a future all unknown,
No opening could I see,
I heard without the night wind moan,
The ways were dark to me,—
" I cannot face it all alone
O be Thou near to me ! "

I had done sums, and sums, and sums,
Inside my aching head.
I'd tried in vain to pierce the glooms
That lay so thick ahead.
But two and two will not make five,
Nor will do when I'm dead.

And then I thought of Him who fed
Five thousand hungry men,
With five small casual loaves of bread,—
Would He were here again !—
Dear God ! hast Thou still miracles
For the troubled sons of men ?

He has, He will, He worketh still,
In ways most wonderful.
He drew me from the miry clay,

He filled my cup quite full.
And while my heart can speak I'll tell
His love unspeakable.

" Rest in the Lord ! "—I saw it there,
On the tablets of the night.
And, comforted, I dropped my care
Where burdens have no weight.
Then, trustfully, I turned and slept,
And woke, and it was light.

God works to-day as He did of old
For the lightening of men's woes.
His wonders never can be told,
His goodness no man knows,—
His Love, His Power, His Tenderness,—
Nor shall do till life's close.

His kindness is so very great,
His greatness is so good.
He looks upon my low estate,
He gives me daily food.
And nothing is too small for Him,—
Yes, truly ! God is good.

Props.

Earthly props are useless,
      On Thy grace I fall;
Earthly strength is weakness,
      Father, on Thee I call,—
      For comfort, strength, and guidance,
      O, give me all !

The Prince of Life.

O, Prince of Life, Thy Life hath tuned
All life to sweeter, loftier grace !
Life's common rounds have wider bounds
Since Thou hast trod life's common ways.

O, Heart of Love ! Thy Tenderness
Still runs through life's rem test vein ;
And lust and greed and soulless creed
Shall never rule the world again.

O Life of Love !—The Good Intent
Of God to man made evident,—
All down the years, despite men's fears,
Thy Power is still omnipotent.

O Life ! O Love ! O Living Word !—
Rent Vail, revealing God to man,—
Help, Lord ! Lest I should crucify,
By thought or deed, Thy Love again.

Judgment Day.

Every day is Judgment Day,
Count on no to-morrow.
He who will not, when he may,
Act to-day, to-day, to-day,
Doth but borrow
Sorrow.

H

Darkness and Light.

There is darkness still, gross darkness, Lord,
On this fair earth of Thine.
There are prisoners still in the prison-house,
Where never a light doth shine.
There are doors still bolted against Thee,
There are faces set like a wall ;
And over them all the Shadow of Death
Hangs like a pall.

> *Do you hear the voices calling,*
> *Out there in the black of the night ?*
> *Do you hear the sobs of the women,*
> *Who are barred from the blessed light ?*
> *And the children,—the little children,—*
> *Do you hear their pitiful cry ?*
> *O brothers, we must seek them,*
> *Or there in the dark they die !*

Spread the Light ! Spread the Light !
Till earth's remotest bounds have heard
The glory of the Living Word ;
Till those that see not have their sight ;
Till all the fringes of the night
Are lifted, and the long-closed doors
Are wide for ever to the Light.
Spread—the—Light !

> *O then shall dawn the golden days,*
> *To which true hearts are pressing ;*
> *When   earth's   discordant   strains   shall*
> *   blend—*
> *The one true God confessing ;*

When Christly thought and Christly deed
Shall bind each heart and nation,
In one Grand Brotherhood of Men,
And one high consecration.

India.

A land of lights and shadows intervolved,
A land of blazing sun and blackest night,
A fortress armed, and guarded jealously,
With every portal barred against the Light.

A land in thrall to ancient mystic faiths,
A land of iron creeds and gruesome deeds,
A land of superstitions vast and grim,
And all the noisome growths that Darkness
breeds.

Like sunny waves upon an iron-bound coast,
The Light beats up against the close-barred
doors,
And seeks vain entrance, yet beats on and on,
In hopeful faith which all defeat ignores.

But—time shall come, when, like a swelling
tide,
The Word shall leap the barriers, and The
Light
Shall sweep the land; and Faith and Love
and Hope
Shall win for Christ this stronghold of the
night.

Livingstone.

To lift the sombre fringes of the Night,
To open lands long darkened to the Light,
To heal grim wounds, to give the blind new
    sight,
  Right mightily wrought he.
        Forth to the fight he fared,
        High things and great he dared,
        He thought of all men but himself,
        Himself he never spared.
        He greatly loved—
        He greatly lived—
        And died right mightily.

Like Him he served, he walked life's troublous
    ways,
With heart undaunted, and with calm, high
    face,
And gemmed each day with deeds of sweetest
    grace ;
  Full lovingly wrought he.
        Forth to the fight he fared,
        High things and great he dared,
        In His Master's might, to spread the
            Light,
        Right lovingly wrought he.
        He greatly loved—
        He greatly lived—
        And died right mightily.

Like Him he served, he would not turn aside ;
Nor home nor friends could his true heart
 divide ;
He served his Master, and naught else beside,
 Right faithfully wrought he.
  Forth to the fight he fared,
  High things and great he dared,
  In His Master's might, to spread the
   Light,
  Right faithfully wrought he.
  He greatly loved—
  He greatly lived—
  And died right mightily.

He passed like light across the darkened land,
And dying, left behind him this command,
"The door is open ! So let it ever stand !"
 Full mightily wrought he.
  Forth to the fight he fared,
  High things and great he dared,
  In His Master's might, to spread the
   Light,
  Right mightily wrought he.
  He greatly loved—
  He greatly lived—
  And died right mightily.

Livingstone the Builder.

With a will !
With a will !
With a will and surely !
Without fail,
Drive each nail,
Build we so, securely !

The Pioneer,—the Undaunted One,
Worn with long journeyings through the
    Great Dark Land,
Rests for a season from his mighty labours,
And seeks fresh vigour in a change of toil.

Labour is sweet,
    When hands and hearts are willing,—
Who truly works
    Is God's own law fulfilling.

With his own hands he helps to build a temple,
Here, in the wilds, a temple to his God,
Rough-hewn and roughly thatched, but still
    a house
Of prayer, a holy place, and consecrate
To Him whose noblest temples are not built
With hands, but in the opened hearts of men.

The Master worked,
    With His own hands expressing
His sure belief
    That therein lay God's blessing.

Thus, as he toils, with axe, and nail, and
    hammer,
His heart rejoices,—so the Master worked,
And by His lowly toil for ever stamped
True labour with its highest dignity.

> *With a will !*
> *With a will !*
> *With a will and surely !*
> *Without fail,*
> *Drive each nail,*
> *Build we so, securely !*

Livingstone's Soliloquy.

"My heart to-day
Is strangely full of home !
How is it
With the dear ones over there ?
    Five years !
    Five long-drawn years !
    And one short moment is enough
      To alter life's complexion for eternity !
Home ! Home ! Home !

   .   .   .   .

    How is it with you all
    At Home ?

   .   .   .   .

And you, my dearest one,
Are ever nearer to me than the rest

Your body lies
    Beneath the baobab
    In far Shapanga ;
But your soul is ever nearest
    When I need you most.
Where a man's treasure is
    His heart is.
And half my heart is buried there with you,
And half works on for Africa.
        Home ! Home ! Home !

    •   •   •   •

Why should such thought of home
        Drag at my heart to-day ?
        Why should I longer roam ?
        Why should I not go home ?
Five years of toilsome wanderings
        May claim a rest !

    •   •   •

        Nay ! God knows best !
        When He sees well
He'll take me home and give me well-earned
        rest.
        The work is not yet done.
        This land of Night
Is not yet fully opened to the Son
        And His fair Light.
        But—when the work is done—
Ah—then !—how gladly will I go—
        Home !—Home !—Home !—
        To rest ! "

Kapiolani.

Where the great green combers break in
    thunder on the barrier reefs,—
Where, unceasing, sounds the mighty diapason
    of the deep,—
Ringed in bursts of wild wave-laughter,
    ringed in leagues of flying foam,—
Long lagoons of softest azure, curving beaches
    white as snow,
Lap in sweetness and in beauty all the isles of
    Owhyhee.

Land more lovely sun ne'er shone on than
    these isles of Owhyhee,
Spendthrift Nature's wild profusion fashioned
    them like fairy bowers ;
Yet behind—below the sweetness,—under-
    neath the passion-flowers,
Lurked grim deeds, and things of horror,
    grisly Deaths, and ceaseless Fears,
Fears and Deaths that walked in Darkness,
    grisly Deaths and ceaseless Fears.

NOTE.—Kapiolani — pronounced Kah-pee-o-lah-ny, with
    slight accent on second syllable.
    Mauna Loa—Mona Lo-ah.
    Kilauea—Kil-o-ee-ah.
    Hale-Mau-Mau—Ha-lee-Mah-oo-Mah-oo.

On the slope of Mauna Loa, in the pit of
    Kilauea,
In the lake of molten lava, in the sea of living
    fire,
In the place of Ceaseless Burnings, in her
    home of Wrath and Terror,
Dwelt the dreadful goddess Pélé—Pélé of the
    Lake of Fire ;
Pélé of the place of torment, Pélé of the Lake
    of Fire.

In the dim far-off beginnings, Pélé flung the
    islands up
From the bottom of the ocean, from the dark-
    some underworld ;
Built them for a house to dwell in, built them
    for herself alone,
So she claimed them and their people, claimed
    them as her very own,
And they feared her, and they worshipped—
    Pélé, the Remorseless One.

But, at times, when she lay sleeping, under-
    neath the lake of fire,
They forgot to do her reverence, they forgot
    the fiery one ;
Then in wrath the goddess thundered from
    the Lake of Ceaseless Burnings,
Flamed and thundered in her anger, till the
    very skies were red,
Poured black ruin on the island, shook it to
    its rocky bed.

Then in fear the people trembled and be-
thought them of their sins,
And the great high priest of Pélé came like
Death down Mauna Loa,
Came to soothe the awful goddess, came to
choose the sacrifice,
Chose the fairest youth or maiden, pointed
with a deadly finger,
Led them weeping up the mountain, victims
to the Lake of Fire.

On the snowy beach of coral, youths and
maidens full of laughter,
Flower-bedecked and full of laughter, sported
gaily in the sun ;
Up above, the slender palm-trees swung and
shivered in the trade-wind,
All around them flowers and spices,—red
hibiscus, sweet pandanus,
And behind, the labouring mountain groaned
and growled unceasingly.

> *" Sea and sunshine,*
> *Care is moonshine,*
> *All our hearts are light with laughter.*
> *We are free*
> *As sun and sea,*
> *What care we for what comes after ? "*

Bride.

"Life was sweet before Love found her,
In his faery bowers.

Life is sweeter,
And completer,
Since he found her,
There, and crowned her
With his fadeless flowers."

Bridegroom.

"Love sought long before he found her,
Ne'er was love like ours !
Long he sought her,
Ere he caught her.
But he found her
There, and bound her
With his fadeless flowers."

"Gaily sporting,
Pleasure courting,
Nought know we of care or sorrow.
We are free
As sun and sea,
What care we what comes to-morrow ? "

Louder still and louder, Pélé roars within her
  lake of fire,
And the youths and maidens trembling look
  in fear up Mauna Loa,
Dreading sight of that grim figure stalking
  down the mountain side ;
For when Pélé claims her victims none the
  summons may avoid.
Pélé calls for whom she chooses—whom she
  chooses goes,—and dies.

See ! He comes ! They start in terror. There,
    along the mountain side,
Death comes stalking, slowly, surely,—*Pélé
must be satisfied.*
Which among them will he summon, with his
    dreadful pointing finger ?
All their hearts become as water, all their
    faces blanch with fear,
Deaths they suffer in the waiting, while dread
    Death draws near.

Now he stands in dreadful menace, seeking
    with a baleful eye
For the sweetest and the fairest—for the
    meetest sacrifice.
" Choose, O choose ! "—they cry in terror ;
    " choose your victim and be gone,
For we each die deaths while waiting, till
    dread Pélé's choice be known !
Choose your victim, Priest of Pélé, choose
    your victim and be gone ! "

Slowly points the dreadful finger, marks the
    newly-wedded bride ;
All the rest, save one, fall from her, as the
    living from the dead.
From the first of time's beginnings Pélé ne'er
    has been gainsayed ;
Pélé chooses whom she chooses, each and all
    the choice abide,
For the common good and safety,—*Pélé must
be satisfied !*

Still the mountain reels and shudders, still
 the awful thunders peal,
Like a snake the ruthless finger holds them
 all in terror still ;
One is there whose life is broken, parted from
 his chosen bride,
But the threatening finger, heedless of the
 lives it may divide,
Lights upon a tiny maiden,—*Pélé must be
 satisfied !*

Slow, the grim high-priest of Pélé turns to
 climb the mountain side ;
Slow, the victims turn and follow,—*Pélé
 must be satisfied.*
All the rest shrink, dumb and helpless, dar-
 ing not to lift an eye,
While above, the labouring mountain cracks
 and belches living fires,
Till the island reels and shudders at dread
 Pélé's agonies.

But a greater one than Pélé walked the
 mountain side that day ;—
To them, climbing, dumb and dim-eyed—
 like a flash of heavenly flame,
Swift and bright as saving angel, fair
 Kapiolani came,
Swiftly as a saving angel, gleaming like a
 heavenly flame,
Thirsting like a sword for battle, fair
 Kapiolani came.

Radiant with the faith of martyrs, all aglow
    with new-born zeal,
Burning to release the people from the bond-
    age and the thrall,
From the deadly thrall of Pélé, from the ever-
    threatening doom,
From the everlasting menace, from the awful
    lake of fire,
Like a bright avenging angel fair Kapiolani
    came !

" Hear me now, you priest of Pélé, and ye
    men of Owhyhee !
Hearken ! ye who cringe and tremble, at the
    sound of Kilauea,
Fearful of the wrath of Pélé, fearful of the
    lake of fire !—
Priest, I say there is no Pélé ! Pélé is not—
    never was !
Pélé lives but in your legends—there is only
    one true God ! "

" Curséd, thrice accurséd, you who thus great
    Pélé do defy,
Here, upon her sacred mountain, of a surety
    you shall die !
Pélé, mighty Pélé, Vengeance ! Strike her
    with thy dreadful doom !
So let every scoffer perish !—Pélé ! Pélé !
    Pélé ! come ! "
And Kapiolani answered—" Pélé ! Pélé !
    Pélé ! come ! "

Loud the mountain roared and thundered ;
    shuddered all who heard and saw,
Dauntless stood Kapiolani, dauntless with
    her faithful few.
" Come ! " she cried again. " Come, Pélé !
    Smite me with thy dreadful doom !
I am waiting, mighty Pélé !—Pélé ! Pélé !
    Pélé ! come ! "
And the mountain roared and thundered ;
    —but the goddess did not come.

" Hearken, Priest ! You have deceived us.
    All your life has been a lie,
Black your heart is, red your hands are, with
    the blood of those who die.
All these years you have misled us with your
    awful threats of doom.
Now it ends ! I do defy you, and your goddess
    I defy.
Pélé, is not, never has been. All your
    worship is a lie.

I will climb your sacred mountain. I will
    dare your lake of fire.
I will eat your sacred berries. I will dare
    your goddess there,
There and then to wreak her vengeance, then
    and there to come in fire,
And with awful burnings end me, now and for
    eternity ;
But if Pélé does not end me, then her worship
    ends this day."

Then the great high priest of Pélé turned to
    fiery Kilauea.
" Come ! " he said, " the goddess calls you ! "
    —and they climbed the mountain side,
Up the slopes of Mauna Loa, to the hell of
    Kilauea,
With the bright blue sky above them, with
    the blazing sun above them,
While the mountain shook beneath them, and
    its head was wrapped in fire.

Fearful, hopeful, all the people crept along
    the shaking path,
Hardly breathing at their daring, thus to
    brave dread Pélé's wrath,
Bending low lest she should see them, breath-
    ing soft lest she should hear,
Certain that Kapiolani would be sacrificed
    that day,
To the vengeance of the goddess, to the anger
    of Pélé.

        " *As little child*
          On mother's breast,
          O rest, my heart,
          Have rest !
          Who rests on Him
          Is surely blest.
          So rest, my heart,
          Have rest !

> *As warrior bold*
> *His foes among,*
> *Be strong, my heart,*
> *Be strong !*
> *Who rests on Him*
> *Shall ne'er go wrong.*
> *Be strong, my heart,*
> *Be strong ! "*

Thus, Kapiolani, dauntless, singing softly as
  she went,
With a face as calm and fearless as a child on
  pleasure bent,
Climbed the side of Mauna Loa, to the dread-
  ful lake of fire,
While the mountain shook and thundered,
  while the people blanched and shuddered,
Climbed to Halé-Mau-Mau,—to the dreadful
  lake of fire.

All the people waited trembling, stood afar
  off pale and trembling,
While Kapiolani, fearless, climbed up to the
  lake of fire,
With the fiery glow all round her, with a
  heavenly light about her.
Shining with a radiance brighter than since
  time began had shone
From the Lake of Ceaseless Burnings, from
  the dreadful lake of fire.

"Here," she cried, "I pluck your berries,
    Pélé,—and I give you none !
See ! I eat your sacred berries, Pélé,—and I
    give you none !
Pélé, here I break your tabus ! Come, with
    all your dreadful fires !
Burn me, Pélé ! I defy you !—Pélé ! Pélé !
    Pélé ! come !
Come now, Pélé, or for ever own that you are
    overcome !

"Pélé comes not. Is she sleeping ? Is she
    wandering to-day ?
Is she busy with her burnings ? Has the
    goddess nought to say ?
Hear me, friends !—There is no Pélé ! One
    true God alone there is.
His, this mountain ! His, these burnings !
    You, and I, and all things,—His !
Goodness, Mercy, Loving-Kindness, Life
    Eternal—all are His !

"From this day, let no man tremble, when he
    feels the mountain shake !
From this day, no man or maiden shall be
    killed for Pélé's sake !
From this day, we break the thraldom of the
    dreadful lake of fire.
From this day, we pass for ever from the
    scourge of Pélé's rod.—
From this day, Thou, Lord Jehovah, be our
    one and only God ! "

They Come!

From North and South, and East and West,
    They come!
The sorely tried, the much oppressed,
Their Faith and Love to manifest,
    They come!
They come to tell of work well done,
They come to tell of kingdoms won,
To worship at the Great White Throne,
    They come!
In a noble consecration,
With a sound of jubilation,
    They come! They come!

Through tribulations and distress,
    They come!
Through perils great and bitterness,
Through persecutions pitiless,
    They come!
They come by paths the martyrs trod,
They come from underneath the rod,
Climbing through darkness up to God,
    They come!
Out of mighty tribulation,
With a sound of jubilation,
    They come! They come!

From every land beneath the sun,
    They come!
To tell of mighty victories won ;
Unto the Father through the Son,
    They come!

They come—the victors in the fight,
They come—the blind restored to sight,
From deepest Darkness into Light ;
    They come !
In a holy exaltation,
With a sound of jubilation,
    They come ! They come !

Processionals.

NORTH.

We come from the gloom of the shadowy trail,
  Out away on the fringe of the Night,
Where no man could tell, when the darkness
    fell,
  If his eyes would behold the light.
      To—the—Night,—
      To—the—Night,—
    To the darkness and the sorrow of the
    Night,—
      Came—the—Light,
      Came—the—Light,
    Came the Wonder and the Glory of the
    Light.

There are wanderers still, without ever a
    guide,
  Out there on the fringe of the Night,
They are bond and blind,—to their darkness
    resigned,

With never a wish for the Light.
        To—their—Night,—
        To—their—Night,—
To the darkness and the sorrow of their
    Night,
        Take—the—Light !
        Take—the—Light !
Take the Wonder and the Glory of the
    Light !

SOUTH.

We come from the land of the blazing sun,
    From the land that was blacker than
        night,—
From the white-hot sand of the Great Dark
    Land,
    Where Might was the only Right.
        To—the—Night,—
        To—the—Night,—
    To the darkness and the sorrow of the
        Night,
            Came—the—Light,
            Came—the—Light,
    Came the Wonder and the Glory of the
        Light.

There are sorrows still, there is darkness still
    There are still gross wrongs to set right ;
There are grim black stains, there are peoples
    in chains,
    To be loosed from the grip of the Night.

To—their—Night,—
To—their—Night,—
To the darkness and the sorrow of their
Night,
Take—the—Light !
Take—the—Light !
Take the Wonder and the Glory of the
Light !

EAST.

We come from the East, from the glowing
East,
Where the Past, with its hand of ice,
Still reaches across through its ages of loss,
And still holds the land like a vice.
To—the—Night,—
To—the—Night,—
To the darkness and the sorrow of the
Night,—
Came—the—Light,
Came—the—Light,
Came the Wonder and the Glory of the
Light.

O, the sorrowful ones of the caste-bound
lands,
How they long for the wider way !
How they sigh in the gloom of their close-
barred tomb
For the Light of the Coming Day !

To—their—Night,—
To—their—Night,—
To the darkness and the sorrow of their
Night,
Take—the—Light,
Take—the—Light !
Take the Wonder and the Glory of the
Light !

WEST.

We come from the Isles, from the Western
Isles,
From the isles of the sunny seas,—
Where the smiles and the wiles, with which
Nature beguiles,
Are but shrouds for her tragedies.
To—the—Night,—
To—the—Night,—
To the darkness and the sorrow of the
Night,—
Came—the—Light,
Came—the—Light,
Came the Wonder and the Glory of the
Light.

There is Darkness more deadly than Death
itself,
There is Blindness beyond that of sight ;
There are souls fast bound in the depths
profound
Of unconscious and heedless Night.

To—their—Night,—
To—their—Night,—
To the darkness and the sorrow of their
Night,
Take—the—Light !
Take—the—Light !
Take the Wonder and the Glory of the
Light !

Faith.

Lord, give me faith !—to live from day to day,
With tranquil heart to do my simple part,
And, with my hand in Thine, just go Thy way.

Lord, give me faith !—to trust, if not to
know ;
With quiet mind in all things Thee to find,
And, child-like, go where Thou wouldst have
me go.

Lord, give me faith !—to leave it all to Thee,
The future is Thy gift, I would not lift
The vail Thy Love has hung 'twixt it and me.

"I Will !"

Say once again Thy sweet "I will ! "
In answer to my prayers.
" Lord, if Thou wilt ? "—
—" I will
Rise up above thy cares ! "

A Little Te Deum of the Commonplace.

A Fragment.

With hearts responsive
And enfranchised eyes,
We thank Thee, Lord,—
For all things beautiful, and good, and true ;
For things that seemed not good yet turned
    to good ;
For all the sweet compulsions of Thy will
That chased, and tried, and wrought us to
    Thy shape ;
For things unnumbered that we take of right,
And value first when first they are withheld ;
For light and air ; sweet sense of sound and
    smell ;
For ears to hear the heavenly harmonies ;
For eyes to see the unseen in the seen ;
For vision of The Worker in the work ;
For hearts to apprehend Thee everywhere ;
           We thank Thee, Lord !

For all the wonders of this wondrous world ;—
The pure pearl splendours of the coming day,
The breaking east,—the rosy flush,—the
    Dawn,—
For that bright gem in morning's coronal,
That one lone star that gleams above the
    glow ;

For that high glory of the impartial sun,—
The golden noonings big with promised life ;
The matchless pageant of the evening skies,
The wide-flung gates,—the gleams of Para-
    dise,—
Supremest visions of Thine artistry ;
The sweet, soft gloaming, and the friendly
    stars ;
The vesper stillness, and the creeping shades ;
The moon's pale majesty ; the pulsing dome,
Wherein we feel Thy great heart throbbing
    near ;
For sweet laborious days and restful nights ;
For work to do, and strength to do the work ;
               We thank Thee, Lord !

For those first tiny, prayerful-folded hands
That pierce the winter's crust, and softly
    bring
Life out of death, the endless mystery ;—
For all the first sweet flushings of the Spring ;
The greening earth, the tender heavenly blue;
The rich brown furrows gaping for the seed ;
For all Thy grace in bursting bud and leaf,—
The bridal sweetness of the orchard trees,
Rose-tender in their coming fruitfulness ;
The fragrant snow-drifts flung upon the
    breeze ;
The grace and glory of the fruitless flowers,
Ambrosial beauty their reward and ours ;
For hedgerows sweet with hawthorn and
    wildrose ;

For meadows spread with gold and gemmed
　　with stars ;
For every tint of every tiniest flower ;
For every daisy smiling to the sun ;
For every bird that builds in joyous hope ;
For every lamb that frisks beside its dam ;
For every leaf that rustles in the wind ;
For spiring poplar, and for spreading oak ;
For queenly birch, and lofty swaying elm,
For the great cedar's benedictory grace ;
For earth's ten thousand fragrant incenses,—
Sweet altar-gifts from leaf and fruit and
　　flower ;
For every wondrous thing that greens and
　　grows ;
For wide-spread cornlands,—billowing golden
　　seas ;
For rippling stream, and white-laced waterfall;
For purpling mountains ; lakes like silver
　　shields ;
For white-piled clouds that float against the
　　blue ;
For tender green of far-off upland slopes ;
For fringing forests and far-gleaming spires ;
For those white peaks, serene and grand and
　　still ;
For that deep sea—a shallow to Thy love ;
For round green hills, earth's full benignant
　　breasts ;
For sun-chased shadows flitting o'er the plain;
For gleam and gloom ; for all life's counter-
　　change ;

For hope that quickens under darkening skies;
For all we see ; for all that underlies,—
We thank Thee, Lord !

For that sweet impulse of the coming Spring,
For ripening Summer, and the harvesting ;
For all the rich Autumnal glories spread,—
The flaming pageant of the ripening woods ;
The fiery gorse, the heather-purpled hills ;
The rustling leaves that fly before the wind,
And lie below the hedgerows whispering ;
For meadows silver-white with hoary dew ;
For sheer delight of tasting once again
That first crisp breath of winter in the air ;
The pictured pane ; the new white world
    without ;
The sparkling hedgerow's witchery of lace ;
The soft white flakes that fold the sleeping
    earth ;
The cold without, the cheerier warmth within ;
For red-heart roses in the winter snows ;
For all the flower and fruit of Christmas-tide ;
For all the glowing heart of Christmas-tide ;
We thank Thee, Lord !

For all Thy ministries,—
For morning mist, and gently-falling dew ;
For summer rains, for winter ice and snow ;
For whispering wind and purifying storm ;
For the reft clouds that show the tender blue ;
For the forked flash and long tumultuous roll;

For mighty rains that wash the dim earth
    clean ;
For the sweet promise of the seven-fold bow ;
For the soft sunshine, and the still calm night ;
For dimpled laughter of soft summer seas ;
For latticed splendour of the sea-borne moon;
For gleaming sands, and granite-frontled
    cliffs ;
For flying spume, and waves that whip the
    skies ;
For rushing gale, and for the great glad calm ;
For Might so mighty, and for Love so true,
With equal mind,
              We thank Thee, Lord !

For maiden sweetness, and for strength of
    men ;
For love's pure madness and its high estate ;
For parentage—man's nearest reach to Thee ;
For kinship, sonship, friendship, brotherhood
Of men—one Father—one great family ;
For glimpses of the greater in the less ;
For touch of Thee in wife and child and friend;
For noble self-denying motherhood ;
For saintly maiden lives of rare perfume ;
For little pattering feet and crooning songs ;
For children's laughter, and sweet wells of
    truth ;
For sweet child-faces and the sweet wise
    tongues ;
For childhood's faith that lifts us near to
    Thee

And bows us with our own disparity ;
For childhood's sweet unconscious beauty
    sleep ;
For all that childhood teaches us of Thee ;
            We thank Thee, Lord !

For doubts that led us to the larger trust ;
For ills to conquer ; for the love that fights ;
For that strong faith that vanquished axe
    and flame
And gave us Freedom for our heritage ;
For clouds and darkness, and the still, small
    voice ;
For sorrows bearing fruit of nobler life ;
For those sore strokes that broke us at Thy
    feet ;
For peace in strife ; for gain in seeming loss ;
For every loss that wrought the greater gain ;
For that sweet juice from bitterness out-
    pressed ;
For all this sweet, strange paradox of life ;
            We thank Thee, Lord !

For friends above; for friends still left below;
For the rare links invisible between ;
For Thine unsearchable greatness ; for the
    vails
Between us and the things we may not know;
For those high times when hearts take wing
    and rise
And float secure above earth's mysteries ;
For that wide, open avenue of prayer,

All radiant with Thy glorious promises ;
For sweet hearts tuned to noblest charity ;
For great hearts toiling in the outer dark ;
For friendly hands stretched out in time of
    need ;
For every gracious thought and word and
    deed ;
          We thank Thee, Lord !

For songbird answering song on topmost
    bough ;
For myriad twitterings of the simpler folk ;
For that sweet lark that carols up the sky ;
For that low fluting on the summer night ;
For distant bells that tremble on the wind ;
For great round organ tones that rise and fall,
Entwined with earthly voices tuned to
    heaven,
And bear our hearts above the high-arched
    roof ;
For Thy great voice that dominates the whole,
And shakes the heavens, and silences the
    earth ;
For hearts alive to earth's sweet minstrelsies ;
For souls attuned to heavenly harmonies ;
For apprehension, and for ears to hear,—
          We thank Thee, Lord !

For that supremest token of Thy Love,—
Thyself made manifest in human flesh ;
For that pure life beneath the Syrian sky—

The humble toil, the sweat, the bench, the
    saw,
The nails well-driven, and the work well-
    done ;
For all its vast expansions ; for the stress
Of those three mighty years ;
For all He bore of our humanity ;
His hunger, thirst, His homelessness and
    want,
His weariness that longed for well-earned
    rest ;
For labour's high ennoblement through Him,
Who laboured with His hands for daily bread;
For Lazarus, Mary, Martha, Magdalene,
For Nazareth and Bethany ;—not least
For that dark hour in lone Gethsemane ;
For that high cross upraised on Calvary ;
The broken seals,—the rolled-back stone—
    The Way,
For ever opened through His life in death ;
For that brief glimpse vouchsafed within the
    vail ;
For all His gracious life ; and for His Death,
With low-bowed heads and hearts impas-
    sionate,
               We thank Thee, Lord !

For all life's beauties, and their beauteous
    growth ;
For Nature's laws and Thy rich providence ;
For all Thy perfect processes of life ;
For the minute perfection of Thy work,

K

Seen and unseen, in each remotest part ;
For faith, and works, and gentle charity ;
For all that makes for quiet in the world ;
For all that lifts man from his common rut ;
For all that knits the silken bond of peace ;
For all that lifts the fringes of the night,
And lights the darkened corners of the earth
For every broken gate and sundered bar ;
For every wide-flung window of the soul ;
For that Thou bearest all that Thou hast
        made ;
                    We thank Thee, Lord !

For perfect childlike confidence in Thee
For childlike glimpses of the life to be ;
For trust akin to my child's trust in me ;
For hearts at rest through confidence in Thee;
For hearts triumphant in perpetual hope ;
For hope victorious through past hopes ful-
        filled ;
For mightier hopes born of the things we
        know ;
For faith born of the things we may not
        know ;
For hope of powers increased ten thousand
        fold ;
For that last hope of likeness to Thyself,
When hope shall end in glorious certainty ;
            *—With quickened hearts
            That find Thee everywhere,
            We thank Thee, Lord !*

Policeman X.

If he would but dare.

I stood, unseen, within a sumptuous room,
Where one clothed all in white sat silently.
So sweet his presence that a pure soft light
Rayed from him, and I saw—most wondrous
    sight !—
The Love of God shrined in the flesh once
    more,
And glowing softly like a misted sun.
His back was towards me. Had I seen his
    face
Methought I must have fallen. I was wrong.
The door flung wide. With hasty step
Came one in royal robes and all the pride
And pomp of majesty, and on his head
A helmet with an eagle poised for flight.
He stood amazed at sight of him in white,
His lips apart in haughty questioning.
But no words came. Breathless, he raised
    his hand
And gave salute as to a mightier lord,

NOTE.—This was written in 1898, at the time of the Tzar's
    Rescript to the Powers suggesting a Peace Conference
    with a view to the lightening of the ever-growing
    burden of arms.
      The possibilities have changed their faces, but at
    heart the great problem remains much the same. And
    above all, the great fact remains that if Great Britain,
    Germany, Russia, and the United States joined hands
    for a World Peace, they could ensure it. Germany is
    still mistrustful. On her lies a great responsibility.

And doffed his helm, and stood. And in his
    eyes I saw
The reflex glory of his Master's face.

The Master spoke. His voice so soft and
    sweet
Thrilled my heart's core and shook me where
    I stood,—
    "Time runs apace. The New Time is at
      hand.
    Shall it be Peace or War ?   It rests with
      THEE."
In dumb amaze the other shook his head.
    "Thy brother of the North has cast his lot
    For peace.   Alone he cannot compass it.
    Shall it be Peace or War ?   It rests with
      THEE."
Again the other shook his head amazed,
But never swerved a hair's breadth in his gaze.
    " Shall it be Peace or War ?   Join hands
      with him,
    Thy Northern brother, with the Western
      Isles,
    And with their brethren of the Further West,
    And Peace shall reign to Earth's remotest
      bound."
And still the other shook his head amazed.
    "Shall it be Peace or War ?   Millions of
      lives
    Are in thy hand, women and men and those
    My little ones. Their souls are mine. Their
      lives

Are in thy hand.   Of thee I shall require
  them.
Shall it be Peace or War ? "

.   .   .   .

.   " I am but one,"
The other answered with reluctant tongue.
"*Thou art* THE *one and so I come to thee.*
For Peace or War the scales are in thy hand.
As thou decidest now, so shall it be.
But,—as thou sayest now, so be it
With thee—then.
Shall it be Peace or War ?   Nay—look !—"
And at the word—where stood the wall—a
  space ;
And at their feet, like mighty map unrolled,—
The kingdoms of the earth, and every king-
  dom
Groaned with the burden of its armour-plate.
And the weight grew till man was crushed
  beneath,
And lost his manhood and became a cog
To roll along the great machine of war.
And, as he watched, the War-Lord's eyes
  flamed fire,
His nostrils panted like a mettled steed's.
This was the game of games he knew and
  loved,
And every fibre of his soul was knit
To see what passed.
              Then,—in a sun-white land,
Where a great sea poured out through
  narrow gates

To meet a greater,—came the clang of arms,
And drew the nations like a tocsin peal,
Till all the sun-white sands ran red, and earth
Sweat blood, and writhed in fiery ashes, and
Grew sick with all the reek and stench of war,
And heaven drew back behind the battle-
    clouds.
And ever, through the clamour of the strife,
I heard the ceaseless wailing of a child,
And the sobbing, sobbing, sobbing, endless
Sobbing of a reft and broken woman ;—
And the hoarse whisper of the War-Lord's
    voice,—

> " Britain fights once again for Barbary
> Lest others occupy to her undoing.
> And Italy and Greece and Turkey join,
> To beat back France and Spain."

Again I saw,—
Where legions marched and wound 'mid
    snowy peaks,
And came upon a smiling vine-clad land,
And filled it with the reek and stench of war.
The hoarse voice spoke,—

> " The provinces she stole
> And lost, Austria takes back."

Again I saw,—
Where white-capped hosts crept swiftly to
    the straits
'Twixt old and new, and drenched the land
    with blood,
And filled it with the reek and stench of war.
The War-Lord spoke,—

" Despite his love of peace,
Our brother of the North has
seized his chance,
And got his heart's desire."
Again I saw,—
Where legions poured through the eternal
snows,
And legions swept o'er every sea to meet
Their long-expected onslaught, and the dead
Were piled in mountains, and the snows ran
red.
The War-Lord spoke,—
" Up, Britain, up ! Strike home !
Or drop your rod of Empire in the
dust—
One of you dies this day."
Again I saw,—
Beneath us, legions swarming to the West,
Devouring kingdoms till they reached the sea,
And filling all the lands with blood and fire.
The War-Lord gazed, with eyes that blazed
and flamed,
And panted like a soul in torment,—" Mine !
All these are mine ! "
" *Thine, sayest thou ?—Thine now,*
When thou shalt stand before me—then,
I shall require them of thee."
—Thus the voice
Of Him who sat and gazed with sorrowing face,
While all the earth beneath us reeked of war,
And heaven grew dim behind the battle-
clouds.

And ever, through the clamour of the strife,
I heard the ceaseless wailing of a child,
And the sobbing, sobbing, sobbing, endless
Sobbing of a reft and broken woman.
  "Shall it be Peace or War?"
A two-edged sword
Could cut no sharper than the gentle voice
Of Him who bowed with sorrow at the sight
Of man destroying man for sake of gain.
I waited, breathless, for the warrior's word.
But no word came. His heart was with his men.
  *"Shall it be Peace or War? Look yet
      again!"*
And at their feet, like mighty map unrolled,
Lay all the kingdoms of the earth—at peace.
The glad earth smiled beneath a smiling
      heaven,
And brought forth fruit for all her children's
      needs.
The desert lands had blossomed, and the earth
Was large enough for all. Her voice came up,
A softly-rounded murmur of content,
Like bees that labour gladly on the comb.
The reign of Peace,—and yet an army lay
Couchant and watchful, ready for the strife
If strife need be,—the strife of quelling
      strife,—
An army culled in part from all the lands,
Owning no master but the public weal,
And prompt to quench the first red spark of
      war.
Even as we watched, a frontier turmoil rose,

And therewith rose the army, and the fire
Died out while scarce begun.   The smoke of it
Was scarcely seen, the noise scarce heard ;
  for all
The lands, sore-spent with war, had welcomed
  Peace,
And bowed to mightier forces than their own;
Men cast aside their armour and their arms,
And lived men's lives and were no more
  machines.
  *" Wars shall there be, indeed, till that last
    war*
  *That shall wage war on War and sweep the
    earth*
  Of all war-wagers and of all mankind."
So spake the voice and ceased.   And still we
  gazed,—
A great white building, on its topmost tower
A great white flag, proclaimed a World's
  Tribunal
For the righting of the nations' wrongs.
And that great army answered its behests
And owned allegiance to no other head.
Peace reigned triumphant.   On the quiet air
I heard the merry laughter of the child,
And the great sigh of gratitude that rose
From all the mother-hearts of all the world.
  " Shall it be Peace or War ? "—
              Once more the voice,—
  "To one man is it given to decide.—
  THOU ART THE MAN ! *The scales are in* THY
    hand.

> *Think well, and say,—Shall it be Peace or*
> *War ?*
> *As thou shalt say so shall it be with thee."*

But, ere the answer came, all vanished like
A scrap of paper in a fire of coals.
Then, with a crackling peal, the thick black
 vail
That hangs before the face of men was rent,
And in the instant lightning flash I saw,—

A chamber hung with black and heaped with
 flowers,
Where candles tall flashed white on watchers'
 swords.
High on a high-raised bier lay one at rest—
Crosses and orders on his quiet breast,
Head proudly cushioned on his country's flag,
Hands calmly folded on his helmet's crest,
His back to earth, his mute face turned to
 heaven,—
Answering the summons of his Over-Lord.
I strained my eyes upon his face to learn
Thereon his answer.   But the dark vail
 dropped,
And left me wondering what his word had
 been.
Had I but read his face I should have known
Who lay there.—Man, like other men ?   Or
 one
Who grasped the greater things, and by his will
Brought Peace on Earth and drew Earth
 nearer Heaven.

The bells beat softly on the midnight air
Proclaiming the New Time. Shall it be Peace?
A voice within me cried and would not cease,
"*One man could do it if he would but dare.*"

Your Place.

Is your place a small place?
Tend it with care!—
He set you there.

Is your place a large place?
Guard it with care!—
He set you there.

Whate'er your place, it is
Not yours alone, but His
Who set you there.

In Narrow Ways.

Some lives are set in narrow ways,
By Love's wise tenderness.
They seem to suffer all their days
Life's direst storm and stress.
But God shall raise them up at length,
His purposes are sure,
He for their weakness shall give strength,
For every ill a cure.

Shut Windows.

For the Braile Magazine.

When the outer eye grows dim,
Turns the inner eye to Him,
  Who makes darkness light.
Fairer visions you may see,
Live in nobler company,
And in larger liberty,
  Than the men of sight.

He sometimes shuts the windows but to open
    hidden doors,
Where all who will may wander bold and free,
For His house has many mansions, and the
    mansions many floors,
And every room is free to you and me.

Some—and Some.

Some have much, and some have more,
Some are rich, and some are poor,
Some have little, some have less,
Some have not a cent to bless
Their empty pockets, yet possess
True riches in true happiness.

To some—unclouded skies and sunny days,
To some—gray weather and laborious ways,
To all—Thy Grace,
To those who fall—Thy tenderness.

Bed=Rock.

I have been tried,
Tried in the fire,
And I say this,
As the result of dire distress,
And tribulation sore—
That a man's happiness doth not consist
Of that he hath, but of the faith
And trust in God's great love
These bring him to.
Nought else is worth consideration.
For the peace a man may find
In perfect trust in God
Outweighs all else, and is
The only possible foundation
For true happiness.

After Work.

Lord, when Thou seest that my work is done
Let me not linger on,
With failing powers,
Adown the weary hours,—
A workless worker in a world of work.
But, with a word,
Just bid me home,
And I will come
Right gladly,—
Yea, right gladly
Will I come.

Kapiolani in Rarotongan.

Mr. F. W. Christian, of the Polynesian Society of New Zealand, whose personal acquaintance with the South Sea Islands and their dialects is unique, is translating " Kapiolani " into Rarotongan. He writes—

" I enclose a four-line stanza which, translating your first line—' Where the great green combers break,' etc.—strictly according to East Polynesian ballad-metres, ushers in your great theme.

" ' Kapiolani ' will, I trust, God willing, become a household classic in many of the Eastern Islands, such as Rapa and Manahiki, where the Rarotongan language runs current as a sort of Lingua Franca or Sacred Esperanto, thanks to the magnificent translation of the Bible by the great missionary, John Williams. I have translated the poem most carefully, and as accurately as possible into the peculiar metre and cast of expression which an Eastern Polynesian 'Atu-Pe'e, or Versifier, would immediately grasp as idiomatic. The first lines run thus :—

Tei te ngai mangúngú—anga no te au
   ngaru roro'a
Ki rúnga no te púnga matoato'a
Ngàru kerekere, ŋgáru mamaáta e tini
Ki rúnga no Te 'Akau-Pipíni.

CPSIA information can be obtained at www.ICGtesting.com
Printed in the USA
BVOW02s1819290514

354709BV00002B/359/P